HAL•LEONARD

ESSENTIAL SONGS

PIANO VOCAL GUITAR

Love Standards

ISBN 1-4234-0130-1

HAL•LEONARD®
CORPORATION
7777 W. BLUEMOUND RD. P.O. BOX 13819 MILWAUKEE, WI 53213

SEAFORD, NY 11783

Visit Hal Leonard Online at
www.halleonard.com

CONTENTS

ALL THE THINGS YOU ARE

from VERY WARM FOR MAY

Lyrics by OSCAR HAMMERSTEIN II
Music by JEROME KERN

ALL THE WAY

Words by SAMMY CAHN
Music by JAMES VAN HEUSEN

AS LONG AS HE NEEDS ME

from the Columbia Pictures - Romulus Motion Picture Production of
Lionel Bart's OLIVER!
from the Broadway Musical OLIVER!

Words and Music by
LIONEL BART

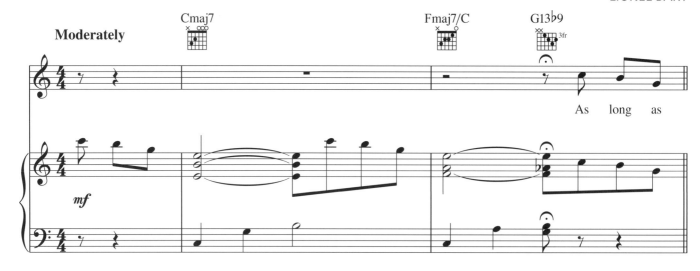

BABY, I'M-A WANT YOU

Words and Music by
DAVID GATES

Oh, it took __ so long to find __ you, ba - by. Ba - by, I'm - a want __ you. Ba - by, I'm - a need you.

Repeat and Fade

CHANGE PARTNERS

from the RKO Radio Motion Picture CAREFREE

Words and Music by
IRVING BERLIN

CAN'T TAKE MY EYES OFF OF YOU

Words and Music by BOB CREWE
and BOB GAUDIO

Moderately

You're just too

good to be true, ___ can't take my eyes off of you. ___ You'd be like
way that I stare, ___ there's noth-ing else to com-pare. ___ The sight of

heav-en to touch, I wan-na hold you so much. At long last
you leaves me weak, there are no words left to speak. But if you

CHANGE THE WORLD

Words and Music by WAYNE KIRKPATRICK,
GORDON KENNEDY and TOMMY SIMS

THE COLOUR OF MY LOVE
from the Musical SCREAM

Words and Music by DAVID FOSTER
and ARTHUR JANOV

I'll paint my mood in shades of blue, ___ paint my soul to be with you. ___
I'll draw your arms a-round my waist ___ then all doubt I shall e-rase. ___

I'll sketch your lips ___ in shad-ed tones, draw your mouth to my
I'll paint the rain ___ that soft-ly lands on your wind-blown

COME RAIN OR COME SHINE
from ST. LOUIS WOMAN

Words by JOHNNY MERCER
Music by HAROLD ARLEN

DREAM A LITTLE DREAM OF ME

Words by GUS KAHN
Music by WILBUR SCHWANDT and FABIAN ANDREE

EASY TO LOVE
(You'd Be So Easy to Love)
from BORN TO DANCE

Words and Music by
COLE PORTER

ERES TU / TOUCH THE WIND

Words and Music by
JUAN C. CALDERON

Slowly

I woke up this morn-ing, and my mind fell a-way,
Co-mo u-na pro-me-sa, e-res tú, e-res tú.

look-ing back sad-ly from to-mor-row.
Co-mo u-na ma-ña-na, de ve-ra-no.

As I heard an ech-o from the
Co-mo u-na son-ri-sa, e-res

past soft-ly say _____ come back, _____ come back, won't you stay?
tú, e-res tú, _____ a-sí, _____ a sí, er-es tú.

EV'RY TIME WE SAY GOODBYE

from SEVEN LIVELY ARTS

Words and Music by
COLE PORTER

FEELINGS
(¿Dime?)

English Words and Music by MORRIS ALBERT
and LOUIS GASTE
Spanish Words by THOMAS FUNDORA

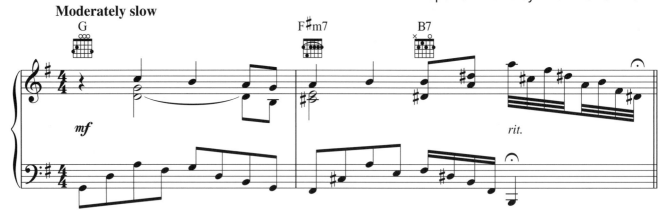

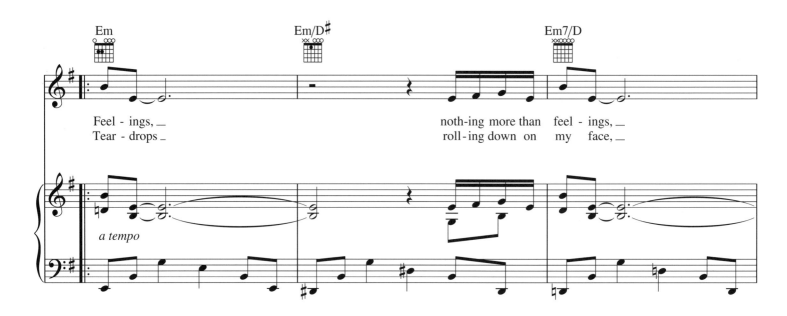

Feel - ings, ___ noth-ing more than feel - ings, ___
Tear - drops ___ roll-ing down on my face, ___

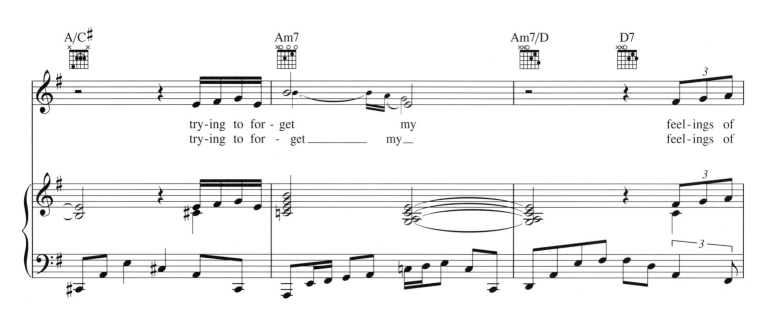

try-ing to for - get my feel-ings of
try-ing to for - get ___ my ___ feel-ings of

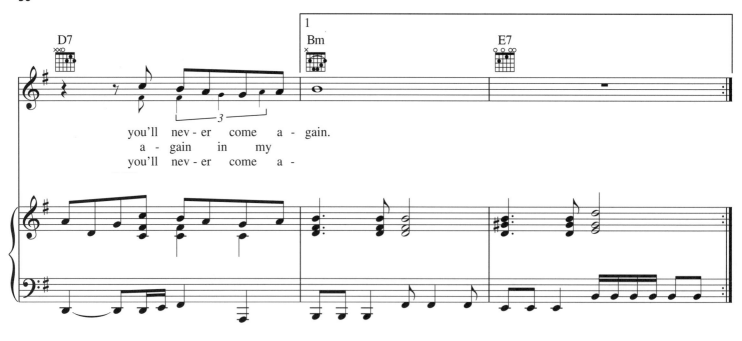

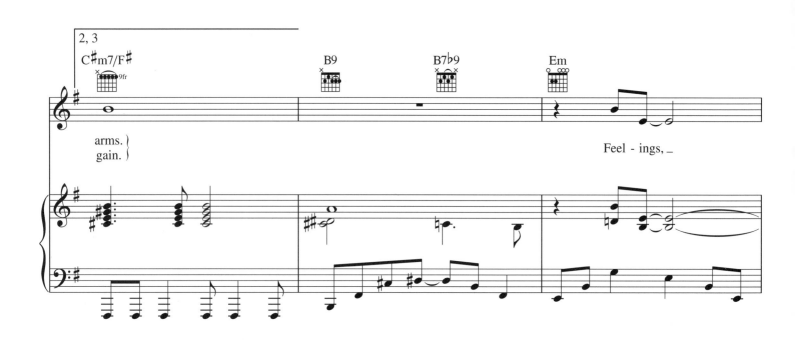

FIELDS OF GOLD

Music and Lyrics by
STING

You'll re - mem - ber me, when the west wind moves _ up a -
stay with me, when will you be my love _ a -

on the fields _ of bar - ley.   You'll for - get the sun in his
mong the fields _ of bar - ley?   We'll for - get the sun in his

FOR ALL WE KNOW

Words by SAM M. LEWIS
Music by J. FRED COOTS

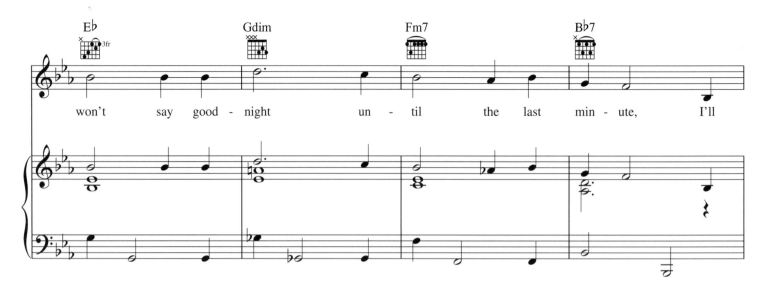

won't say good - night un - til the last min - ute, I'll

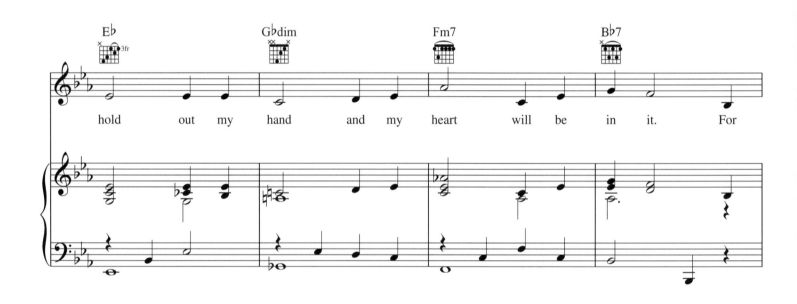

hold out my hand and my heart will be in it. For

all we know this may on - ly be a dream; We

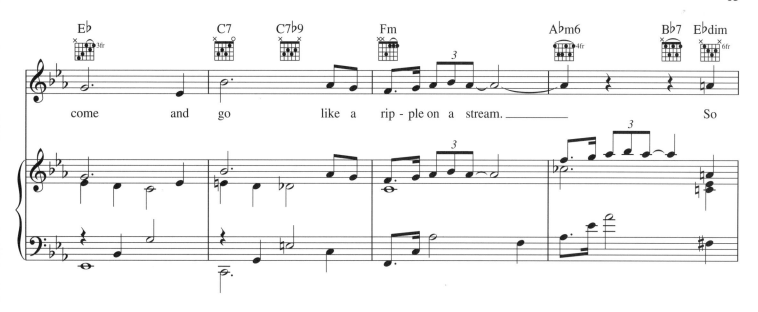

come and go like a rip-ple on a stream. _____ So

love me to-night, to - mor-row was made for some, to -

mor-row may nev-er come, for all we know. _____

FOR ONCE IN MY LIFE

Words by RONALD MILLER
Music by ORLANDO MURDEN

FROM HERE TO ETERNITY

Words by ROBERT WELLS
Music by FRED KARGER

GROW OLD WITH ME

Words and Music by
JOHN LENNON

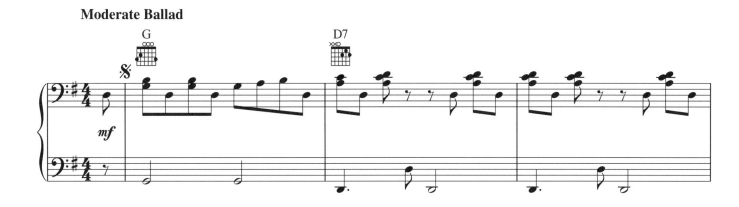

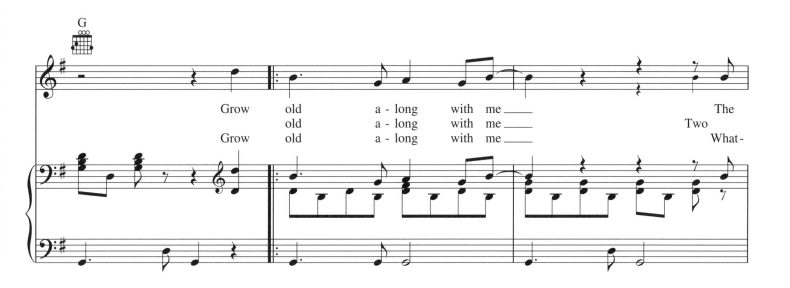

Grow old a - long with me _____ The
old a - long with me _____ Two
Grow old a - long with me _____ What-

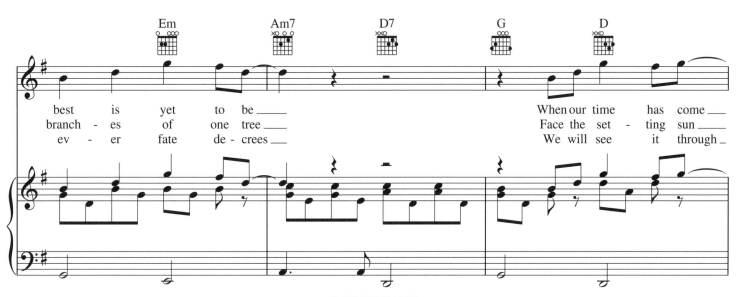

best is yet to be _____ When our time has come _____
branch - es of one tree _____ Face the set - ting sun _____
ev - er fate de - crees _____ We will see it through _

THE GLORY OF LOVE

from GUESS WHO'S COMING TO DINNER
featured in the Motion Picture BEACHES

Words and Music by
BILLY HILL

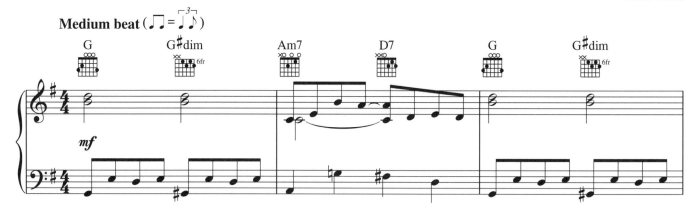

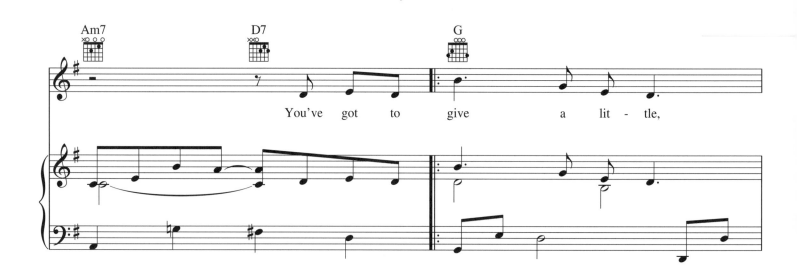

You've got to give a lit-tle,

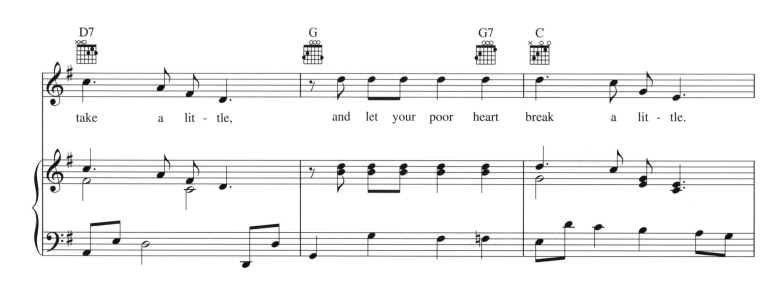

take a lit-tle, and let your poor heart break a lit-tle.

A GROOVY KIND OF LOVE

Words and Music by TONI WINE
and CAROLE BAYER SAGER

When I'm feel-in' blue, all I have to do is take a look at
want to, you can turn me on to an-y-thing you

you, then I'm not so _____ blue. When you're close to me, I can feel your
want to, an-y time at _____ all. When I kiss your lips, oo, I start to

heart beat, I can hear you breath-ing _____ in _____ my _____ ear.
shiv-er, can't con-trol the quiv-er-ing _____ in-side. } Would-n't you a-

HERE, THERE AND EVERYWHERE

Words and Music by JOHN LENNON
and PAUL McCARTNEY

HOW AM I SUPPOSED TO LIVE WITHOUT YOU

Words and Music by MICHAEL BOLTON
and DOUG JAMES

I BELIEVE IN YOU AND ME

from the Touchstone Motion Picture THE PREACHER'S WIFE

Words and Music by DAVID WOLFERT
and SANDY LINZER

I LEFT MY HEART IN SAN FRANCISCO

Words by DOUGLASS CROSS
Music by GEORGE CORY

I CAN'T BELIEVE THAT YOU'RE IN LOVE WITH ME

Words and Music by JIMMY McHUGH
and CLARENCE GASKILL

Yes - ter - day, you came my way. And when you smiled at
Skies are gray, I'm blue each day. When you are not a -

me, in my heart I felt a thrill. _____ You
round, ev - 'ry - thing goes wrong, my dear, _____ I've

me. I just can't i - mag - ine that you love me.

And af - ter all is said and done, to

think that I'm the luck - y one. I can't be - lieve that you're in love with

me. Your

me.

I CAN'T GIVE YOU ANYTHING BUT LOVE

from BLACKBIRDS OF 1928

Words and Music by JIMMY McHUGH
and DOROTHY FIELDS

I DON'T KNOW WHY
(I Just Do)

Lyric by ROY TURK
Music by FRED E. AHLERT

Slowly, with feeling

All day long you're ask-ing me what I see in you. All day long I'm an-swer-ing, but what good does it do? I have noth-ing to ex-plain. I just love you, love you, and I'll tell you once a-gain. I don't know why___ I

I LOVE HOW YOU LOVE ME

Words and Music by BARRY MANN
and LARRY KOLBER

Moderately slow

I love how your eyes close _ when-ev-er you kiss me; _ and when I'm a-
Instrumental

way from you I love how you miss me. _ I love the way you al-ways treat me _ ten-der-

ly; but dar-ling most of all, I love how you love me. _ I love how your
Instrumental ends

I REMEMBER YOU
from the Paramount Picture THE FLEET'S IN

Words by JOHNNY MERCER
Music by VICTOR SCHERTZINGER

I SWEAR

Words and Music by FRANK MYERS
and GARY BAKER

Lyrics under staff:
I see the ques - tions in___ your eyes;___ I know what's weigh -
I'll give you ev - 'ry - thing___ I can;___ I'll build your dreams

I WILL

Words and Music by JOHN LENNON
and PAUL McCARTNEY

I WON'T LAST A DAY WITHOUT YOU

Words and Music by PAUL WILLIAMS
and ROGER NICHOLS

Day af-ter day __ I must face a world __ of stran-gers where I
So man-y times __ when the cit-y seems __ to be with-out a

don't be-long; __ I'm not that strong. It's nice to know __ that there's
friend-ly face, __ a lone-ly place, it's nice to know __ that you'll

some-one I __ can turn to who will al-ways care; __ you're
be there if __ I need you, and you'll al-ways smile; __ it's

al - ways there.
all worth-while.
When there's no get-ting o - ver that rain - bow, __ when my small - est of dreams __ won't come __ true, I can take all the mad - ness the world __ has to give, __ but I won't __ last a day __ with out you. _____

I'LL KNOW
from GUYS AND DOLLS

By FRANK LOESSER

I'LL NEVER LOVE THIS WAY AGAIN

Words and Music by RICHARD KERR
and WILL JENNINGS

I'M STILL IN LOVE WITH YOU

Words and Music by AL GREEN,
WILLIE MITCHELL and AL JACKSON, JR.

I'VE GOT MY LOVE TO KEEP ME WARM

from the 20th Century Fox Motion Picture ON THE AVENUE

Words and Music by
IRVING BERLIN

Bright jump tempo

The snow is snow-ing, the wind is blow-ing, but I can weath-er the storm. What do I care how much it may storm?

I'VE GOT THE WORLD ON A STRING

Lyric by TED KOEHLER
Music by HAROLD ARLEN

Mer - ry month of May, sun - ny

IF YOU ARE BUT A DREAM

Words and Music by NATHAN BONX,
JACK FULTON and MOE JAFFE

I'VE GROWN ACCUSTOMED TO HER FACE

from MY FAIR LADY

Words by ALAN JAY LERNER
Music by FREDERICK LOEWE

IN MY LIFE

Words and Music by JOHN LENNON
and PAUL McCARTNEY

ISN'T IT ROMANTIC?

from the Paramount Picture LOVE ME TONIGHT

Words by LORENZ HART
Music by RICHARD RODGERS

JUST IN TIME

from BELLS ARE RINGING

Words by BETTY COMDEN and ADOLPH GREEN
Music by JULE STYNE

THE LAST WALTZ

Words and Music by LES REED
and BARRY MASON

JUST ONCE

Words by CYNTHIA WEIL
Music by BARRY MANN

Slowly

I did my best, _____ but I
I gave my all, _____ but I

guess my best _ was-n't good _ e-nough _ 'cause here we are, _ back where we were _ be-fore. _
think my all _ may have been _ too much _ 'cause Lord knows we're _ not _ get-ting an - y - where. _

Seems noth-ing ev - er chang - es, we're
It seems we're al - ways blow-in' what-

LET THERE BE LOVE

Lyric by IAN GRANT
Music by LIONEL RAND

LET'S GET LOST

from the Paramount Picture HAPPY GO LUCKY

Words by FRANK LOESSER
Music by JIMMY McHUGH

Let's get lost, _____ lost in each oth- er's

arms. Let's get lost; _____

let them send out a - larms. And though they'll

THE LOOK OF LOVE
from CASINO ROYALE

Words by HAL DAVID
Music by BURT BACHARACH

THE LONG AND WINDING ROAD

Words and Music by JOHN LENNON
and PAUL McCARTNEY

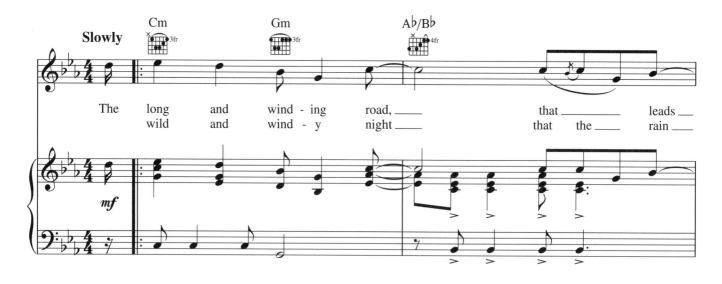

The long and wind-ing road, _____ that _____ leads _____
wild and wind-y night _____ that the _____ rain _____

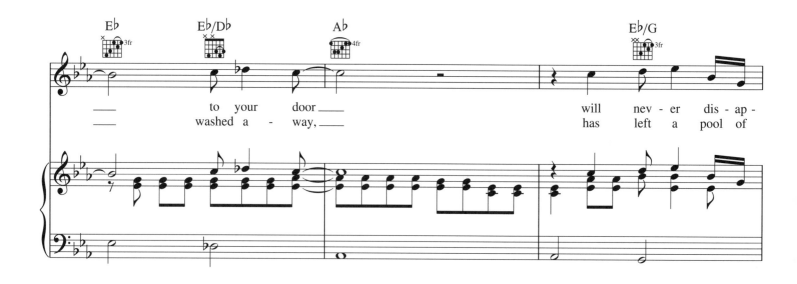

_____ to your door _____
_____ washed a - way, _____

will nev - er dis-ap-
has left a pool of

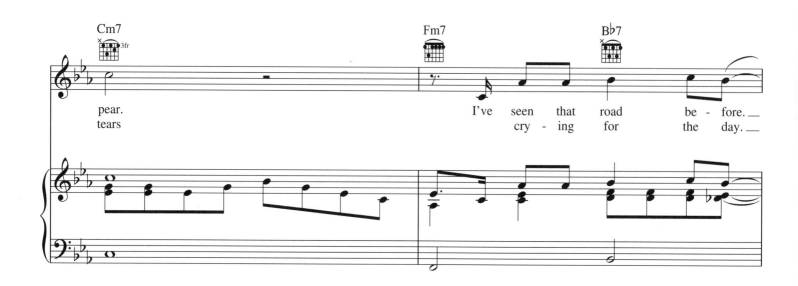

pear.
tears

I've seen that road be-fore. _____
cry - ing for the day. _____

LOVE AND MARRIAGE

Words by SAMMY CAHN
Music by JAMES VAN HEUSEN

LOVE'S IN NEED OF LOVE TODAY

Words and Music by
STEVIE WONDER

LOVE IS A SIMPLE THING

Words by JUNE CARROLL
Music by ARTHUR SIEGEL

LOVE LETTERS
Theme from the Paramount Picture LOVE LETTERS

Words by EDWARD HEYMAN
Music by VICTOR YOUNG

LOVE ME

Words and Music by JERRY LEIBER
and MIKE STOLLER

MORE
(Ti Guarderò Nel Cuore)
from the Film MONDO CANE

Music by NINO OLIVIERO and RIZ ORTOLANI
Italian Lyrics by MARCELLO CIORCIOLINI
English Lyrics by NORMAN NEWELL

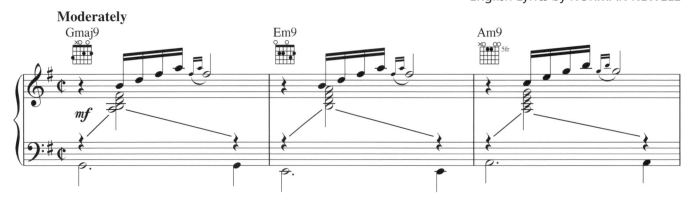

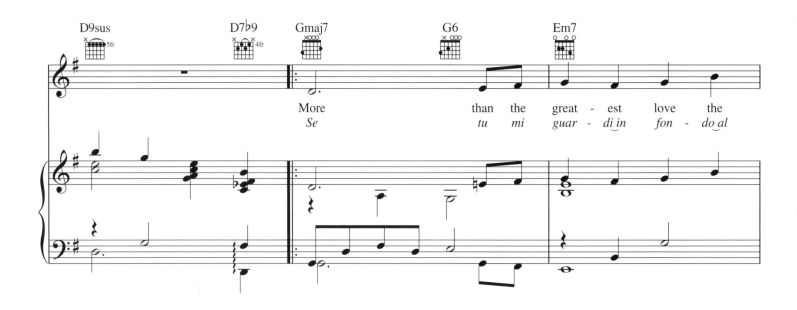

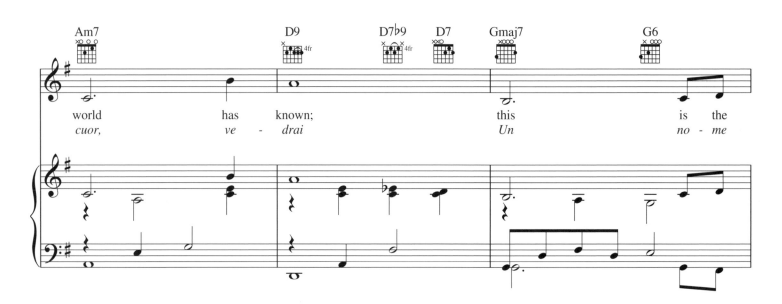

MY CHERIE AMOUR

Words and Music by STEVIE WONDER,
SYLVIA MOY and HENRY COSBY

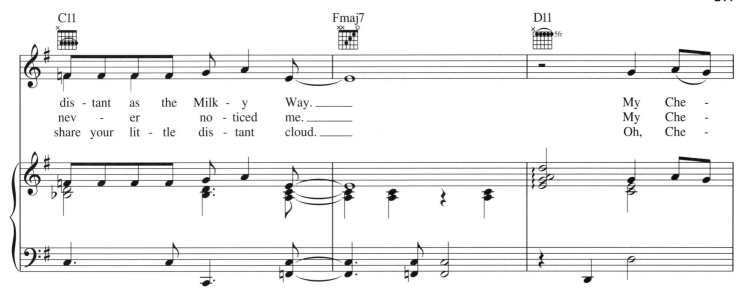

dis - tant as the Milk - y Way._____ My Che -
nev - er no - ticed me._____ My Che -
share your lit - tle dis - tant cloud._____ Oh, Che -

rie A - mour,__ pret - ty lit - tle one that I_____ a - dore,__
rie A - mour,__ won't you tell me how could you____ ig - nore__
rie A - mour,__ pret - ty lit - tle one that I_____ a - dore,__

you're the on - ly girl my heart_____ beats for; __ how I wish that you were mine._
that be - hind that lit - tle smile____ I wore, __ how I wish that you were mine._
you're the on - ly girl my heart_____ beats for; __ how I wish that you were mine._

MY ONE AND ONLY LOVE

Words by ROBERT MELLIN
Music by GUY WOOD

Lyrics:

The ver-y thought of you makes my heart sing __ like an A-pril breeze __ on the wings of spring, and you ap-pear in all your splen-dor, __ my one and on-ly love. The shad-ows fall and spread their

MY HEART STOOD STILL
from A CONNECTICUT YANKEE

Words by LORENZ HART
Music by RICHARD RODGERS

MY PRAYER

Music by GEORGES BOULANGER
Lyric and Musical Adaptation by JIMMY KENNEDY

When the twi-light is gone _____ and no song-bird is sing-ing, _____

_____ when the twi-light is gone _____ you come in-to my

THE NEARNESS OF YOU

from the Paramount Picture ROMANCE IN THE DARK

Words by NED WASHINGTON
Music by HOAGY CARMICHAEL

NEVERTHELESS
(I'm in Love with You)

Words and Music by BERT KALMAR
and HARRY RUBY

NO TWO PEOPLE
from the Motion Picture HANS CHRISTIAN ANDERSEN

By FRANK LOESSER

PEOPLE WILL SAY WE'RE IN LOVE

from OKLAHOMA!

Lyrics by OSCAR HAMMERSTEIN II
Music by RICHARD RODGERS

NOBODY ELSE BUT ME

from the Revival of SHOWBOAT

Lyrics by OSCAR HAMMERSTEIN II
Music by JEROME KERN

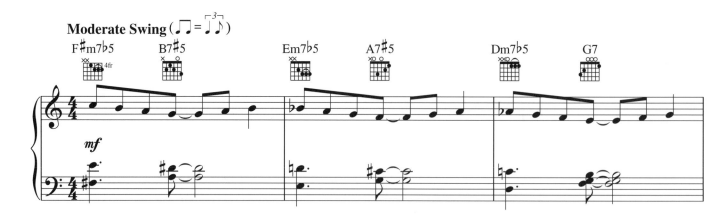

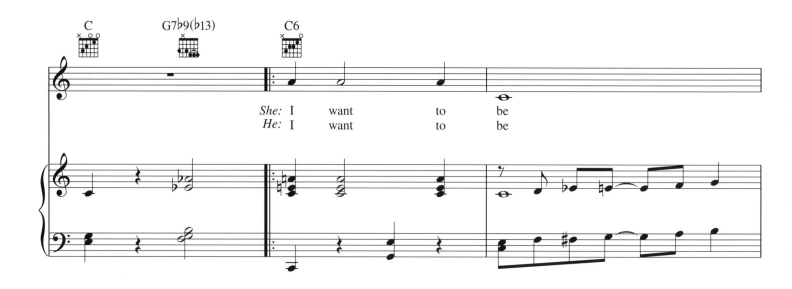

She: I want to be
He: I want to be

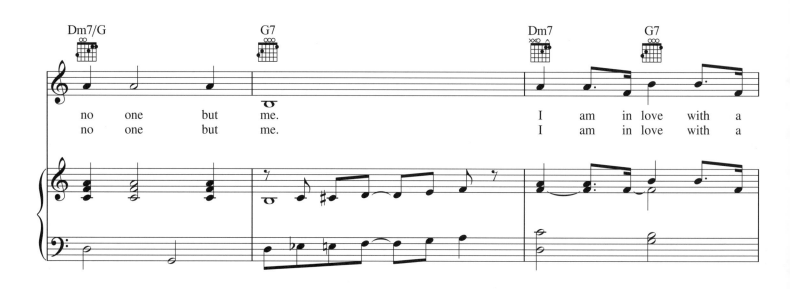

no one but me.
no one but me.

I am in love with a
I am in love with a

ON A SLOW BOAT TO CHINA

By FRANK LOESSER

ONLY YOU
(And You Alone)

Words and Music by BUCK RAM
and ANDE RAND

PRECIOUS AND FEW

Words and Music by
WALTER D. NIMS

REMEMBER

Words and Music by
IRVING BERLIN

REUNITED

Words and Music by DINO FEKARIS
and FREDDIE PERREN

one per-fect fit ___ and, sug-ar, this one is it. ___ We both are so ex-cit-ed, 'cause we're

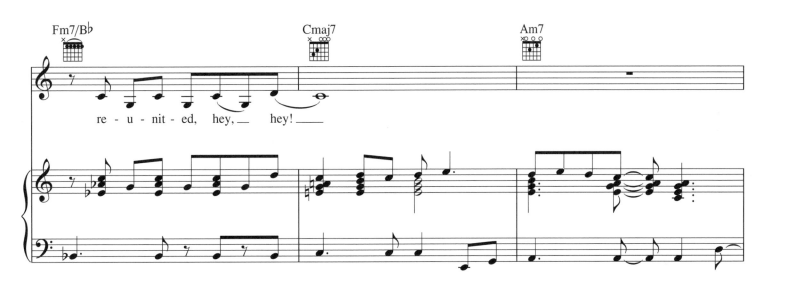

re - u - nit-ed, hey, ___ hey! ___

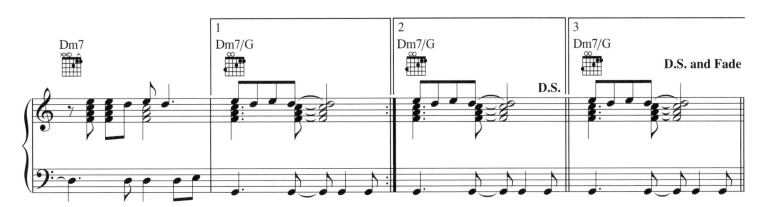

D.S. and Fade

Additional Lyrics

4. Ooh, listen, baby, I won't ever make you cry, I won't let one day go by
Without holding you, without kissing you, without loving you.
Ooh, you're my everything, only you know how to free
All the love there is in me.
I wanna let you know, I won't let you go.
I wanna let you know, I won't let you go.
Ooh, feels so good!

SLEEP WARM

Words and Music by ALAN BERGMAN,
LEW SPENCE and MARILYN KEITH

You're fall- ing a- sleep on my shoul- der, it's a- bout that time a- gain. I'll call you first thing in the morn- ing, dar- ling, till

SO IN LOVE
from KISS ME, KATE

Words and Music by
COLE PORTER

SOFT LIGHTS AND SWEET MUSIC

from the Stage Production FACE THE MUSIC

Words and Music by
IRVING BERLIN

I can't re - sist the moan of a cel - lo,

SOMETIMES WHEN WE TOUCH

Words by DAN HILL
Music by BARRY MANN

STRANGER IN PARADISE

from KISMET

Words and Music by ROBERT WRIGHT
and GEORGE FORREST
(Music Based on Themes of A. Borodin)

TAKE MY BREATH AWAY
(Love Theme)
from the Paramount Picture TOP GUN

Words and Music by GIORGIO MORODER
and TOM WHITLOCK

Watch-ing ev-'ry mo-tion in ___ my fool-ish lov-er's game; ___ on this end-less o-cean, fi-

Watch-ing, I keep wait-ing, still ___ an-tic-i-pat-ing love, ___ nev-er hes-i-tat-ing to ___

Watch-ing ev-'ry mo-tion in ___ this fool-ish lov-er's game; ___ haunt-ed by the no-tion some-

TALK TO ME

Words and Music by EDDIE SNYDER,
RUDY VALEE and STAN KAHAN

TEARS IN HEAVEN

Words and Music by ERIC CLAPTON
and WILL JENNINGS

Be - yond the door ____ there's peace, I'm sure, ____

and I know ___ there'll be no more ___ tears in heav -

en.

TENDERLY
from TORCH SONG

Lyric by JACK LAWRENCE
Music by WALTER GROSS

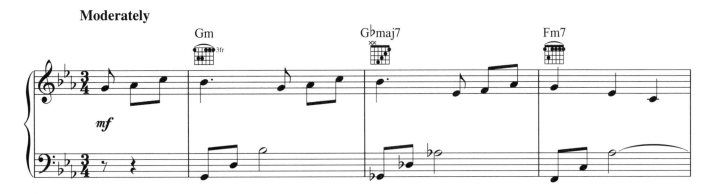

The eve-ning breeze ca-ressed the trees ten-der-ly; ___

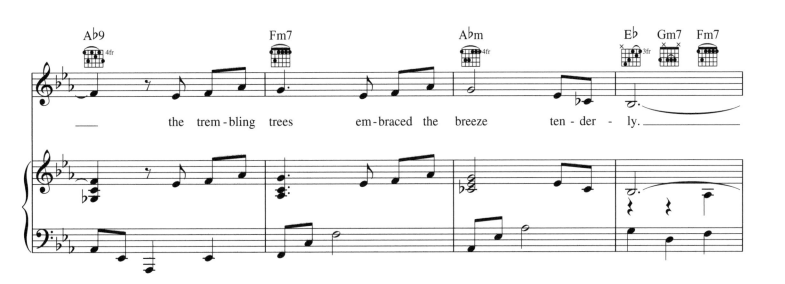

___ the trem-bling trees em-braced the breeze ten-der-ly. ___

THERE'S NO YOU

Words and Music by TOM ADAIR
and HAL HOPPER

I feel _____ the au-tumn breeze, it
lone - ly au-tumn trees, how

steals 'cross my pil-low as soft as a will - o' - the - wisp, _____ and in its
soft - ly they're sigh-ing, for sum-mer is dy - ing, they know _____ that in my

song there is sad - ness be - cause _____ there's no you. The
heart there's no glad - ness be - cause _____

THE THINGS WE DID LAST SUMMER

Words by SAMMY CAHN
Music by JULE STYNE

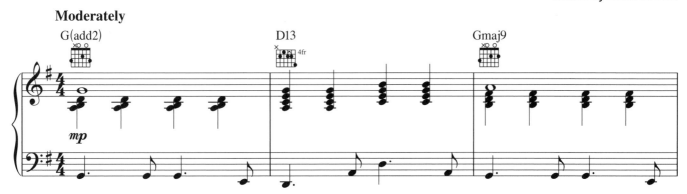

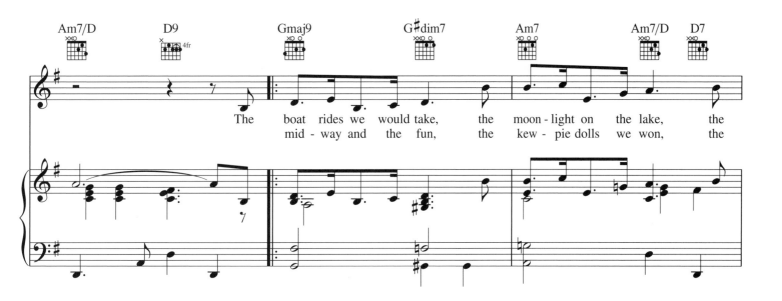

The boat rides we would take, the moon-light on the lake, the

mid - way and the fun, the kew - pie dolls we won, the

way we danced and hummed our fav - 'rite song. The

bell { I / you } rang to prove that { I was / you were } strong. The

THEY SAY IT'S WONDERFUL

from the Stage Production ANNIE GET YOUR GUN

Words and Music by
IRVING BERLIN

Annie: Ru - mors fly and you
Frank: Ru - mors fly and you

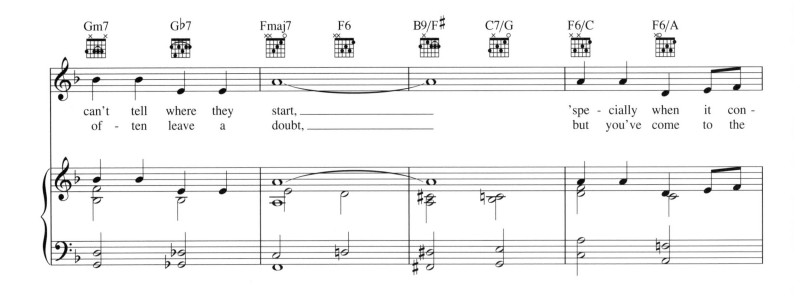

can't tell where they start, _____ 'spe - cially when it con -
of - ten leave a doubt, _____ but you've come to the

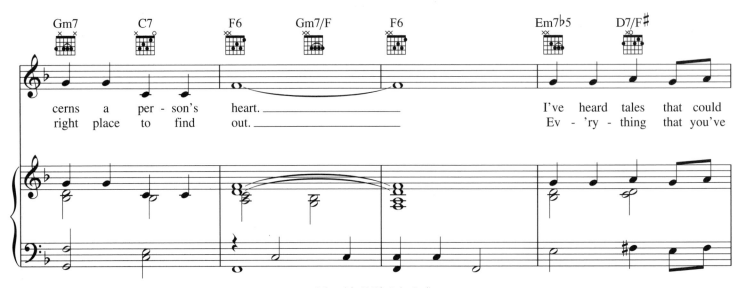

cerns a per - son's heart. _____ I've heard tales that could
right place to find out. _____ Ev - 'ry - thing that you've

Lyrics (upper line / lower line):

say. _____ And with a moon up a - bove, it's
say. _____ *Frank:* And with a moon up a - bove, it's

won - der - ful, _____ it's won - der - ful, _____ so they
won - der - ful, _____ it's won - der - ful, _____ *Annie:* so you

tell me. _____ I can't re - call who said it, I
tell me. _____ *Frank:* To leave your house some morn - ing, and

know I nev - er read it. I on - ly know they
with - out an - y warn - ing, you're stop - ping peo - ple,

THIS GUY'S IN LOVE WITH YOU

Lyric by HAL DAVID
Music by BURT BACHARACH

THIS LOVE OF MINE

Words and Music by SOL PARKER,
HENRY W. SANICOLA and FRANK SINATRA

TILL THERE WAS YOU
from MEREDITH WILLSON'S THE MUSIC MAN

By MEREDITH WILLSON

A TIME FOR US
(Love Theme)
from the Paramount Picture ROMEO AND JULIET

Words by LARRY KUSIK and EDDIE SNYDER
Music by NINO ROTA

TIME IN A BOTTLE

Words and Music by
JIM CROCE

If I could save time in a bottle, the first thing that I'd like to do

I could make days last for - ev - er, if words could make wish - es come true,

TO LOVE AND BE LOVED

from the Film SOME CAME RUNNING

Words by SAMMY CAHN
Music by JAMES VAN HEUSEN

UNEXPECTED SONG
from SONG AND DANCE

Music by ANDREW LLOYD WEBBER
Lyrics by DON BLACK

Gently (♩ = 76)

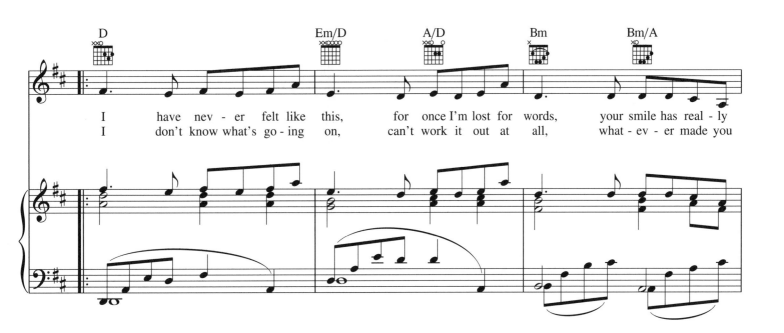

I have nev-er felt like this, for once I'm lost for words, your smile has real-ly
I don't know what's go-ing on, can't work it out at all, what-ev-er made you

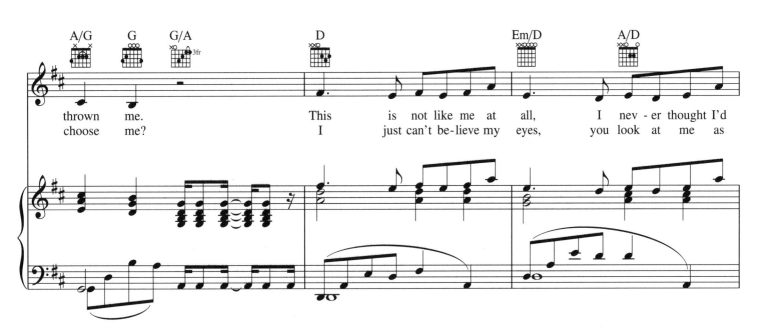

thrown me. This is not like me at all, I nev-er thought I'd
choose me? I just can't be-lieve my eyes, you look at me as

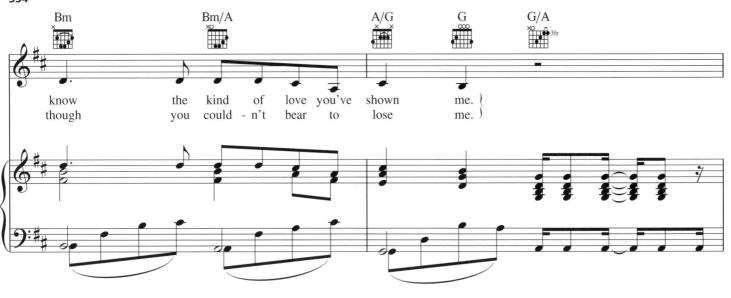

know   the kind of love you've shown   me.
though   you could-n't bear to   lose   me.

Now,   no mat-ter where I am,   no mat-ter what I do,   I see your face ap-

pear-ing   like   an un-ex-pect-ed song,   an un-ex-pect-ed

all, I nev-er thought I'd know the kind of love you've shown me.

Now, no mat-ter where I am, no mat-ter what I do, I see your face ap-

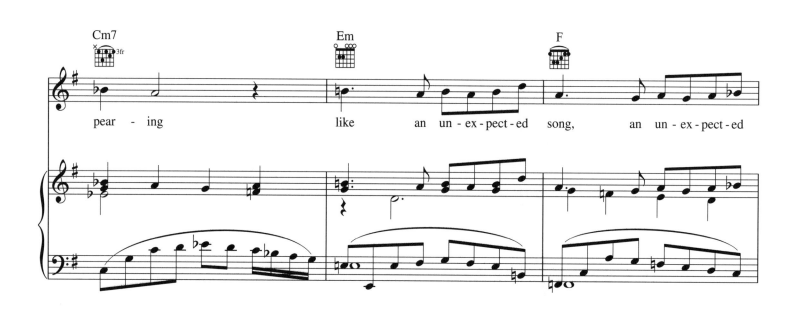

pear - ing like an un-ex-pect-ed song, an un-ex-pect-ed

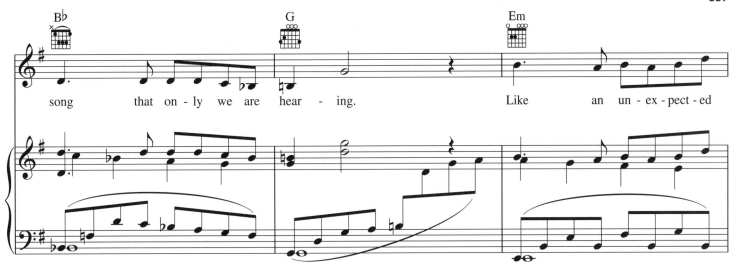

song that on-ly we are hear - ing. Like an un-ex-pect-ed

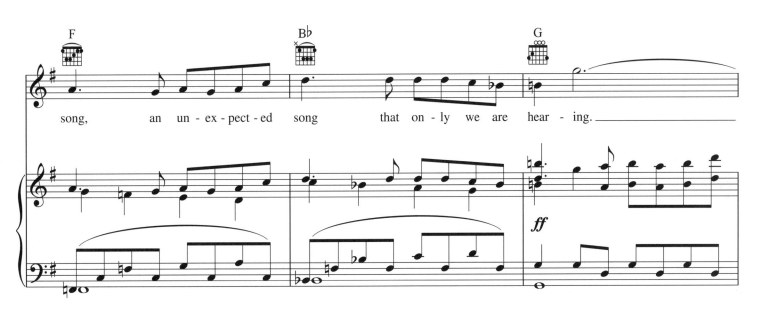

song, an un-ex-pect-ed song that on-ly we are hear-ing.

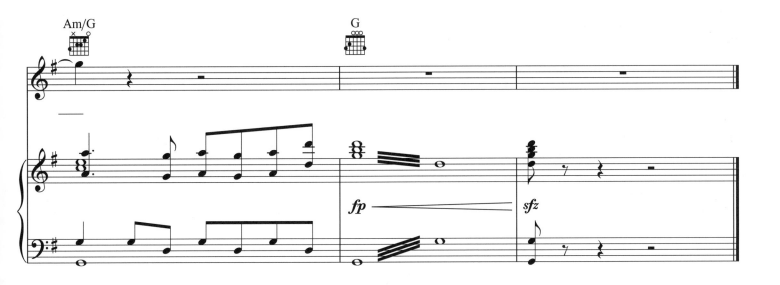

TOP OF THE WORLD

Words and Music by JOHN BETTIS
and RICHARD CARPENTER

Such a feel - in's com - in' o - ver me, _____ there is
Some - thing in ___ the wind has learned my name, _____ and it's

THE TOUCH OF YOUR HAND

from ROBERTA

Words by OTTO HARBACH
Music by JEROME KERN

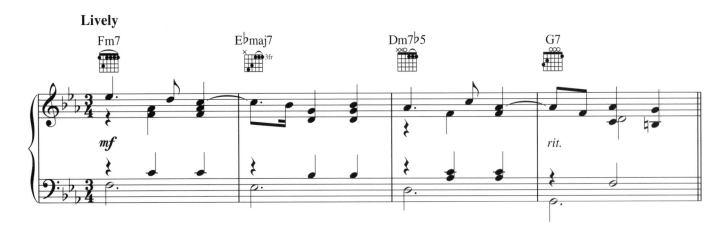

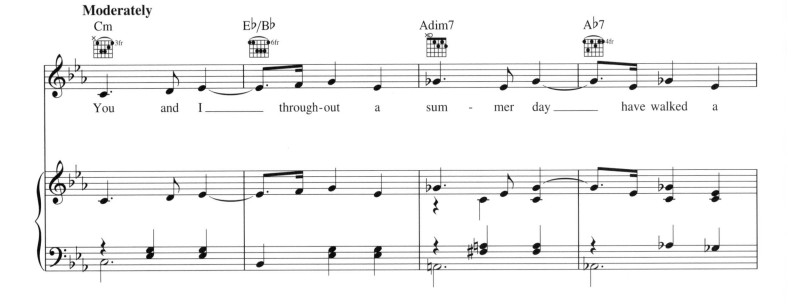

You and I _____ through-out a sum - mer day _____ have walked a

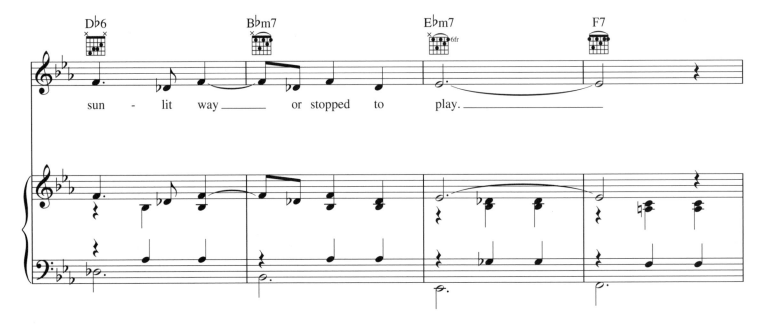

sun - lit way _____ or stopped to play. _____

UNTIL IT'S TIME FOR YOU TO GO
from ELVIS ON TOUR

Words and Music by
BUFFY SAINTE-MARIE

VALENTINE

Words and Music by JACK KUGELL
and JIM BRICKMAN

Smoothly

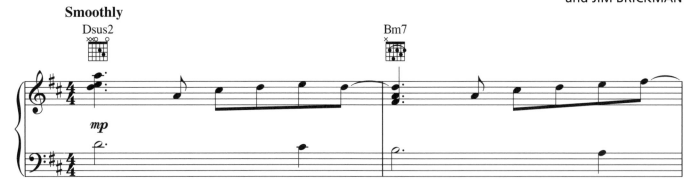

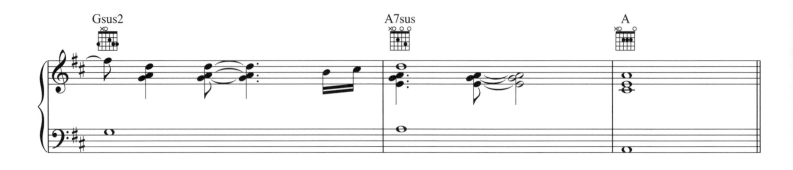

If there were no words, _____ no way to speak, _____ I _____
All of my life, _____ I have been wait - ing for _____ all _____

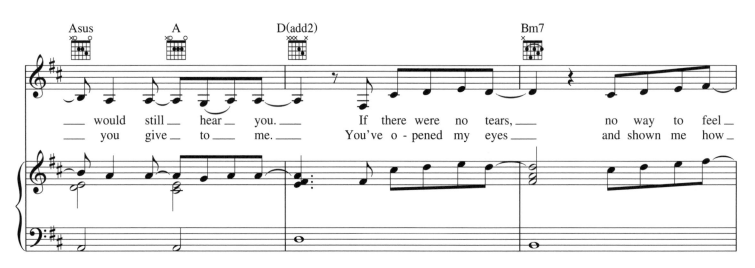

_____ would still _____ hear _____ you. _____ If there were no tears, _____ no way to feel
_____ you give _____ to _____ me. _____ You've o - pened my eyes _____ and shown me how _____

THE VERY THOUGHT OF YOU

Words and Music by
RAY NOBLE

THE WAY WE WERE
from the Motion Picture THE WAY WE WERE

Words by ALAN and MARILYN BERGMAN
Music by MARVIN HAMLISCH

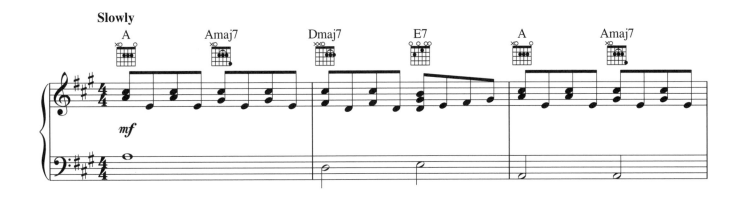

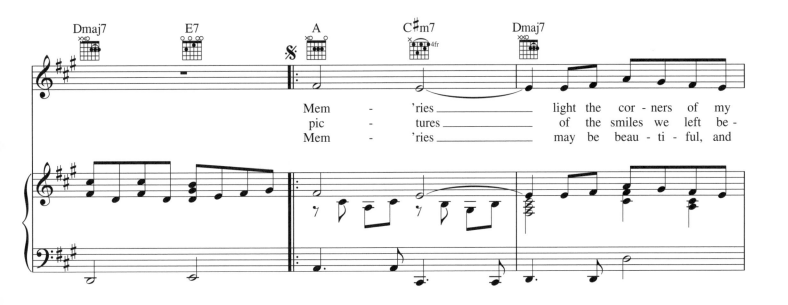

Mem - 'ries _____ light the cor - ners of my
pic - tures _____ of the smiles we left be -
Mem - 'ries _____ may be beau - ti - ful, and

mind.
hind,   Mist - y wa - ter - col - or mem - 'ries _____
yet,   smiles we gave to one an - oth - er _____
          what's too pain - ful to re - mem - ber _____

The Way You Look Tonight

from SWING TIME

Words by DOROTHY FIELDS
Music by JEROME KERN

YOU ARE THE SUNSHINE OF MY LIFE

Words and Music by
STEVIE WONDER

WHAT YOU WON'T DO FOR LOVE

Words and Music by BOBBY CALDWELL
and ALFONS KETTNER

YOU ARE BEAUTIFUL

from FLOWER DRUM SONG

Lyrics by OSCAR HAMMERSTEIN II
Music by RICHARD RODGERS

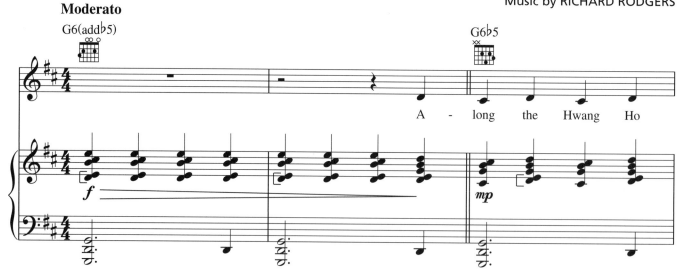

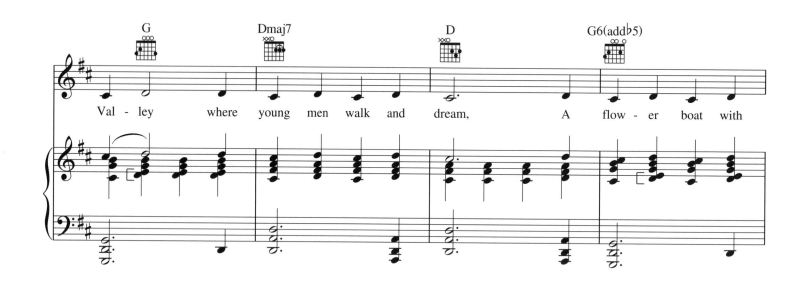

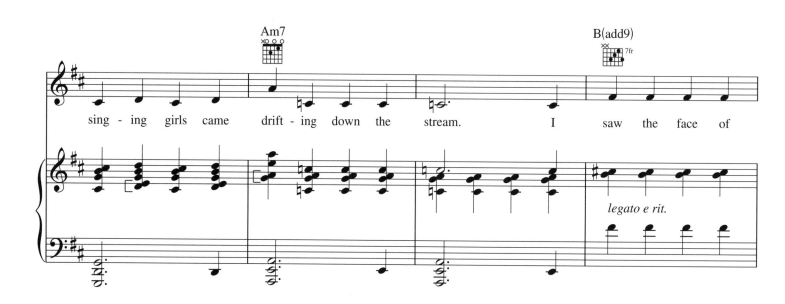

YOU DECORATED MY LIFE

Words and Music by DEBBI HUPP
and BOB MORRISON

YOU, MY LOVE

Words and Music by JAMES VAN HEUSEN
and MACK GORDON